An Introduction to Computable Contracts

Matt Roberts, Dan Selman, Diana Lease, Timothy Tavarez, Tom Brooke, Martin Halford, Niall Roche

Published by Accord Project

Acknowledgements

Peter Hunn for review and feedback.
Alice Roberts for proofreading and copy-editing.

March 2024: First Edition

Notices

All trademarks, logos, and brand names are the property of their respective owners. All company, product and service names used in this paper are for identification purposes only. Use of these names, trademarks and brands does not imply endorsement.

An Introduction to Computable Contracts © 2024, by Accord Project, a Series of LF Projects, LLC. Published under a Creative Commons Attribution licence (CC BY), version 4.0.
ISBN 978-1-304-53524-5

This book is published under a CC BY licence, which means that you can copy, redistribute, remix, transform, and build upon the content for any purpose, even commercially, as long as you give appropriate credit, provide a link to the licence, and indicate if changes were made. Licence details:
creativecommons.org/licenses/by/4.0/

Foreword

Dr. Megan Ma
Assistant Director, Stanford Center for Legal Informatics (CodeX)

Over the last few decades, and perhaps accelerated within the past year by the advent of generative AI and large language models (LLMs), we have begun to explore what human-machine collaboration may look like for the legal space. Yet, the emergence of copilots, augmented "intelligence", rests on an assumption of an unanswered question: how exactly does collaboration look like in legal practice? Unlike other domains where there may be clear analogs of collaboration, there is, in contrast, incredible variability in the legal domain. In fact, collaboration has arguably been hindered by the tools that we have used historically, such that legal work appeared to resemble more of an assembly line, rather than a shared knowledge space.

As such, we have seen the legal community bend to their tools, working within the confines of word processors. For example, because of the library system of checking documents in and out, we maintained a practice of parcelling off individual tasks that are pieces of a whole. Yet, in this age of generative AI, if we continue to think of human-machine collaboration as purely task-oriented, we will lose sight of how value may be generated together.

Perhaps what underpins this problem is a reality that we have no legal metrics to verify how we, as human experts, perform relative to one another. That underscores the messiness of defining human-machine collaboration. Because we do not have these metrics nor have we been encouraged by past tools to collaborate, we simply have been unprepared for what working with technology could really offer. Importantly, we have not considered deeply the comparative advantage between human and machine, nor even amongst machines. Just as working in teams requires understanding the relative strengths of each member, a necessary first step is to explicitly clarify the limitations and historical behaviours of our legal practice and determine how they may be opportunities for our tools. We should also be accounting for interoperability with our existing tools, assessing where our processes and behaviours correlate so that we may connect and bridge multiple machines together.

Accordingly, we are beginning to see how hybrid, or compound[1], systems (symbolic + neural), such as Google Deepmind's AlphaGeometry[2], are driving impact. Applied to legal, we should perhaps reflect on how to enrich legal taxonomies and formal logic of expert systems with the implicit contexts of legal expression.

This is precisely the motivation behind the Accord Project and of the broader computable contracts' community towards the development of Smart Legal Contracts. It is to envision agreements as not a static instantiation and/or representation of a contractual relationship, but instead a dynamic framework that enables contracts to be active (machine) collaborators in the process. Furthermore, Smart Legal Contracts apply longstanding structured data approaches to support the reasoning of unstructured contract information by LLMs. At the same time, high velocity, high volume capabilities of LLMs allow for accelerating intermediary workflows of translating natural language contracts into structured form. In effect, we are seeing both emerging and ongoing efforts to evaluate the relative strengths and limitations of respective tools and gauge how they may together encourage efficiencies across the contract lifecycle.

This whitepaper is emblematic of a practical guide towards achieving meaningful human-machine collaboration, such that our legal and transactional workflows are not only augmented, but built natively for efficiency and transparency.

About Accord Project

Accord Project[3] champions the importance of integrating contract text with computer-code for contractual automation. This paradigm is often referred to as a Computable Contract or Smart Legal Contract.

Founded in 2018, Accord Project is a non-profit, collaborative, initiative developing an ecosystem and open source tools for computable contracts. The community includes participants from law firms, technology companies, universities, government, and private individuals.

Today, the community maintains a technology-neutral foundation for smart legal contracts, based on the combination of legal text with a machine-readable data model, and machine-executable logic. This definition of a smart legal contract is recognised across the industry, including by statutory and standards bodies.

Accord Project is a top-level Linux Foundation[4] project and publishes code using the Apache-2 Open Source licence.

Contents

Foreword..3
About Accord Project...5
Problem Statement..7
    Filling the Contract Gap..7
    Shifting Legal Landscape..8
Transitioning to Smart Legal Contracts...10
    The Case for Machine-readable Contracts..............................10
    The Potential of Artificial Intelligence.......................................12
    Defining a Smart Legal Contract... 16
    Progressive Adoption of Smart Legal Contracts......................23
    Design Decisions...28
    Community & Adoption.. 31
Conclusion...35
Further Information..36
    How to Get Involved..36
Glossary...39
References...43

Problem Statement

Accord Project builds Open Source data formats and foundational software libraries for solutions that fill the contract gap[5]. This section defines the problems that arise from the contract gap and recent industry trends that influence the work of Accord Project.

Filling the Contract Gap

Today, most contracts are drafted as word-processed documents and then either signed on paper, or signed electronically. However the key provisions and data-points within the word-processed text are challenging for machines to extract reliably, and the underlying logic of the contract is even more of a challenge for machines to automate. This means that significant overhead falls on manual human processes to manage, perform, and enforce the contractual terms.

This leads to numerous well-documented inefficiencies in contract management. The IACCM estimates that approximately 9% of the value of all contracts is lost[6] due to inefficient management of contract data.

Most companies manage their contracts as documents (either physical or digital). Laborious human review and oversight is required to answer basic questions about contractual rights and obligations, related issues, such as regulatory compliance, and the other data captured within the contract text. This is costly and time-consuming.

In addition, the lack of a digital representation of the contract (text, data, and logic) makes it challenging to:
- Share contract details with interested third-parties (counterparties to the contract, auditors, or dispute resolution bodies).

- Send contract data to downstream enterprise systems: customer relationship management, human resources, enterprise resource planning, finance etc.
- Get real-time visibility into all the obligations the enterprise has entered into.
- Search, report on, and run analytics across groups of contracts (e.g. with a particular party or parties, expiring between certain dates, for common products sold to customers in a particular geography/jurisdiction).

👁 Read more about the Contract Gap and Contract Value Leakage[7]

Shifting Legal Landscape

The legal world is changing and Legal Tech is a billion dollar industry[8]. The modern lawyer has to be at home in the digital world. Law Schools now teach courses in coding for lawyers, computational law, blockchain, and artificial intelligence. Legal Hackers[9] is a worldwide movement uniting lawyers across the world in a shared passion for law and technology. Lawyers need to move beyond the written word on paper and there is a growing body of publications that describe this transition, including "Smart Legal Contracts: Computable Law in Theory and Practice[10]" co-authored by Peter Hunn (co-founder of Accord Project).

Accord Project is far from alone in working in the Smart Legal Contracts/Computable Contracts domain, and other notable communities are hosted at Stanford CodeX[11] and MIT[12].

In November 2021, the Law Commission of England and Wales concluded[13] that the current legal framework in England and Wales is sufficiently robust and adaptable to be able to facilitate and support the use of smart legal contracts. This legal clarity confirms that smart contracts are legally binding and enforceable agreements, and also sets out the rules for creating, executing and interpreting smart contracts.

> 👁 Read our blog post[14] for more details on the legal status of smart legal contracts and this video[15] for their differences with smart contracts.

There is also a growing community of legal technology companies and communities promoting the use of digital and standardized contracts for document assembly, drafting, review and negotiation.

Notable examples include, oneNDA[16], Common Paper[17], Common Form[18], Standard Draft[19], and Docassemble[20].

These companies and communities (as well as others) are reimagining the contract; not as a word processing document, but as a dynamic digital artefact that is standardized using expert community consensus to provide a shared product benefiting from scaled adoption and that is natively machine-readable. In fact, some of them use the very same tools for distribution of artefacts, such as Git version control, that are used by software communities.

The shift to standardization is a theme similar to industrialization, in which common and relatively low-level building blocks achieve industry acceptance, for example, as has been seen with IETF, W3C, and other organisations.

Transitioning to Smart Legal Contracts

The Case for Machine-readable Contracts

A machine-readable contract has a host of beneficial functionality, including making contracts:
- Searchable.
- Analyzable.
- Real-time.
- Integrated.

The ability to *search* and report on data across sets of contracts allows managers of contracts to more efficiently see an aggregate view across their portfolio of contracts. This allows for finding commonalities across documents to reduce redundancy and address conflicting terms, rights, and obligations. Data can then be used to conclude which contracts and terms lead to beneficial outcomes for the represented party, and which should be changed or removed in future contracts. Contract managers can also answer questions about their contracts more quickly if they are easily searchable.

When contracts are represented as data that can be interpreted by machines, this enables *analyzing* existing and future contracts:

- The performance and outcomes of previous contracts can inform future decisions.
- Scenarios can be run on various combinations of terms to find which combination is the most favourable and these analyses used to author future contracts or make amendments to existing contracts.
- Contracts can be analyzed during the negotiation phase to identify risks before entering into a new contract.

Machine-executable contracts can have access to *real-time* data:

- Parties involved in the contract can respond to changes that affect the terms and obligations of the agreement instantly.
- Conditional clauses can be executed accurately and efficiently based on real-time data being fed into the contract.
- Actions can be triggered as soon as specific conditions are met.

Machine-readable contracts can also be *integrated* with external systems and technologies. This allows the real-time data mentioned above to come from accurate, verifiable sources or IoT devices, resulting in:

- Streamlined workflows with existing business and transaction software.
- Manual and error-prone processes such as redundant data entry can be reduced if a contract is integrated directly with existing systems of record for key business data, such as accounting or human resources.
- Financial obligations can be automated using trusted payment gateways.

Consequently, contracts are transformed from business liabilities in constant need of costly human management, to assets capable of providing business intelligence and value.

A report from the Law Commission[13] also outlined further benefits of adopting smart legal contracts, "through standardization of contracts covering employment, insurance, supply chain, credit, tax, and intellectual property, as well as more complex agreements." Use cases that were highlighted by the report included helping organisations to meet environmental, social, and governance (ESG) commitments by providing transparency and efficiencies in critical supply chains, and by restoring trust in audit and corporate governance.

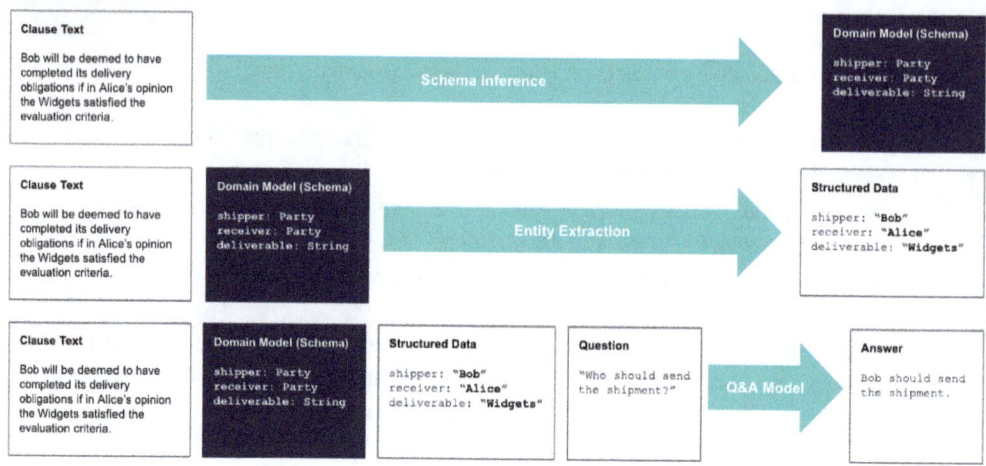

Figure 1: Complementing ML processes with Domain Models

The Potential of Artificial Intelligence

In scenarios where a natively machine-readable document is not available, recent advances in Large Language Models (LLM), Natural Language Processing (NLP), and Machine Learning (ML) can help us to discover the structure and meaning from text automatically.

When we need to extract structured data from unstructured documents, Accord Project data formats are useful to have as the output from ML processes so that we can more easily ingest the documents into other tools. Similarly, structured data formats (called Schemas or Domain Models) can also be used to complement the input for some ML processes (Figure 1).

Finally, domain models and their relationship to entities identified in the contract text provide valuable training data for models to better understand contracts, beyond just plain text and standard entity resolution techniques.

One area where these approaches can be useful is for Question and Answering use cases where natural language or structured questions are asked of the contract to extract relevant information. While LLMs are constantly improving, having more context about the contract using structured data through Accord Project data formats can provide better results than plain text analysis of the contract.

Examples from Industry and Academia

The Accord Project has explored approaches to generate smarter versions of contracts using NLP and LLMs. Specifically, approaches such as retrieval augmented generation (RAG), LLM fine-tuning, and Knowledge Graph creation have shown promising results.

For example, the paper "Conversion of Legal Agreements into Smart Legal Contracts using NLP"[21] is focused on the generation of Accord Project templates and models and the accurate classification of entities and relationships (Figure 2).

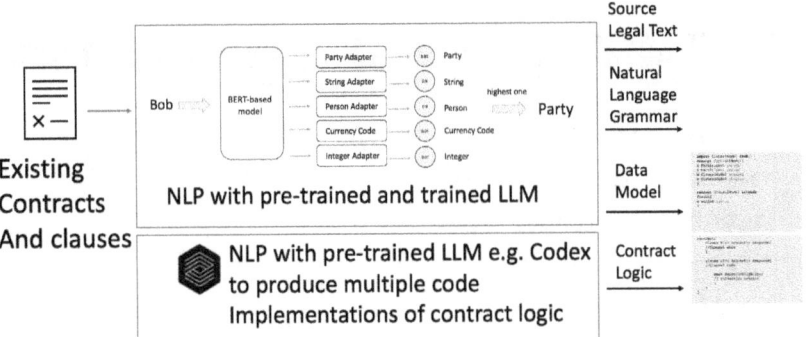

Figure 2: Conversion of Legal Agreements into Smart Legal Contracts using NLP[21]

LLMs can also be used to create domain models from sample contracts, or natural language chat interactions, so-called Schema Inference. For example, see the experimental work from Dan Selman to use LLMs to create Concerto data models via the Finchbot[22] web-service and his blog documenting his experiences[23].

LLMs have also been shown to be good at generating executable programming code; this invites the possibility of automatic codification of legal clauses.

Converting natural language contracts to a code representation through the automatic extraction of obligation logic graphs (OLG) and conversion to Accord Project data structures has been explored by a research paper from Northwestern University and Adobe Research[24]. This approach describes the extraction of key entities, relationships, and formulas into a graph representation called the Obligation Logic Graph (OLG). OLGs allow the semantic meaning of contract obligations, including dependencies between obligations, to be captured and mapped to code downstream.

The longer-term goal of this work is to aid the creation of Smart Legal Contract components from existing contracts and domains, creating reusable SLC components such as clauses and data structures. We hope the approaches developed can be integrated into tools and pipelines for SLC creation.

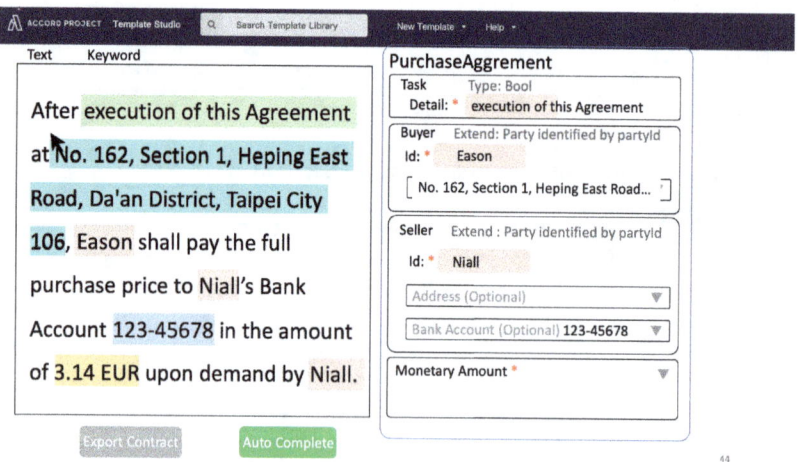

Figure 3: Prototype tool for automated entity extraction from Conversion of Legal Agreements into Smart Legal Contracts using NLP[21]

LLMs can be prone to issues such as hallucinations and there is a need for a 'human in the loop' and the need for a high degree of accuracy in the legal domain compared to other domains where accuracy is less of a concern and outputs are 'good enough'. Ensuring the quality of the output of these models will be a key consideration in any pipeline involving generative models, especially for any data models and code output by models. We see this technology, in this stage of its maturity, as a productivity aid to humans, providing suggestions and starting points, rather than complete ML powered end-to-end automation.

Harnessing the ongoing advances in the capabilities of LLM will continue to be the goal of the Accord Project NLP Working Group and the academic and industrial researchers active in this area.

👁 Read more about applying LLMs to legal technology[25].

Defining a Smart Legal Contract

A Smart Legal Contract (also known as a Computable Contract) is a human-readable and machine-readable contract that is digital, consisting of natural language and computable components.

Smart Legal Contracts are defined by their three high-level components:

1. The Text component includes the contract natural language, formatting information, placeholders for deal-terms ("variables"), and assembly logic.
2. The Model describes the shape of the data used in the Text and by the Logic. Often called a data model, or schema.
3. The Logic captures the contract and template semantics (Contract Definition Logic) in code.

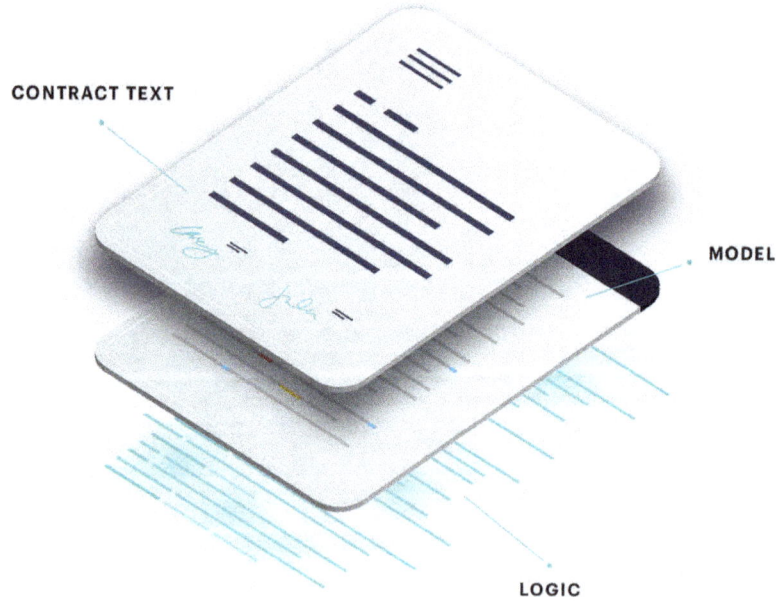

> ● Read about how Smart Legal Contracts are different from blockchain Smart Contracts[26]

Templating and Document Assembly (Text)

Most document assembly systems rely on template engines that are fundamentally text-based — i.e. they treat templates as text strings and in simple terms, perform a "find and replace" operation. This approach creates a coupling between the input format of the template, say, a Word Document (in DOCX format), and the output of the template engine, which in the case of a DOCX template, has to be a DOCX file. This makes supporting multiple input and output formats difficult. For example, many organisations would like to use a single template that can be filled out on their HTML5 website, within a mobile application, and delivered as a PDF.

Given the ability for templates to contain *contract assembly logic* there is a need to ensure that the templates are safe and consistent - i.e. when a template is merged with well-structured data it is guaranteed to produce a well-structured output; we describe this property as *template safety*.

> ● Read more about TemplateMark and Template Engine[29].

Describing Contract Data (Model)

Contracts include data points: the names of parties, addresses, details of purchased products, insurance provisions, warranties, expiration dates etc. To make contract data points machine-readable, a *data model* representation is required. Given Accord Project's platform neutral goals, this data model must be usable across platforms. In addition, to allow computation over the data points in a contract the data modelling language must be usable from a variety of runtime execution environments and programming languages.

The Accord Project sponsors development of the Concerto data modelling language[27], to describe the structure of data in a contract. Concerto models can be converted to a wide variety of platform-specific data models, such as JSON Schema, TypeScript, C#, Java, and Go.

> Read more about the features, goals and motivations for Concerto[28].

Contract Definition Logic

Contracts frequently describe how multiple parties are expected to behave. From a technical standpoint they describe a distributed state-machine or business process, for example, for a sales contract:

1. On signature of the contract the seller must send the goods to the buyer.
2. The buyer then has 30 days to inspect and formally accept the goods.
3. Upon acceptance of the goods, or when the 30 day inspection period has expired, the buyer must send $100 to the seller in exchange for the goods.

Numerous projects exist with the goal of digitizing the logic of contracts, although unfortunately adoption of each has been limited, outside of specific domains. Typically, these projects fit into one of the following categories.

- Domain-specific languages. Developing and maintaining custom programming languages is costly and requires highly specialized engineering skills.
- Distributed ledgers and blockchain.
- Low-code solutions.

⦿ Summary of approaches from ICAIL 2023 : Workshop of Computable Contracts[30]

A key challenge to be resolved is the very high cost of converting the contract text into a computable form, as today it requires highly skilled programmers (or logicians) who are versed in both technology and the legal intent of the contract.

Note

Contract Definition Logic is different from *Contract Assembly Logic*, although both may be implemented in machine-executable code. Contract Definition Logic captures the semantics of a contract, such as the buyer/seller relationship above, whereas Contract Assembly Logic captures the data-driven assembly of the contract. For example, contract assembly logic could determine which clauses to include based on the jurisdiction of the contract, whereas the contract definition logic would determine the conditions for termination.

Similarly, Contract Definition Logic is often distinct from the *Contract Automation Logic* associated with a contract. For example, the Contract Definition Logic defines the value of a payment obligation, but external settlement logic captures how the obligation is fulfilled. Or more concretely, a contract might say, *you must pay $10,000 after signing*, but the operational process to approve, release and transfer $10,000 is defined outside of the contract. Often the Automation Logic is private to one of the parties.

⦿ Read more about the Taxonomy of contract logic[31]

A Simple Example (Fixed Rate Loan)

By combining text and data, a clause or contract becomes machine-readable.

Contract Text

For instance, the clause below for a fixed rate loan[32] includes natural language text coupled with variables. Together, these variables refer to some data for the clause and correspond to the 'deal points':

```
This is a *fixed interest* loan to the amount of {{loanAmount}} at
the yearly interest rate of {{rate}}% with a loan term of
{{loanDuration}},
and monthly payments of {{monthlyPayment}}.
```

Contract Data

To make sense of the data, a *Data Model*, expressed in the Concerto schema language, defines the variables for the template and their associated data types:

```
// loanAmount is a floating-point number
o Double loanAmount

// rate is a floating-point number
o Double rate

// loanDuration is an integer
o Integer loanDuration

// monthlyPayment is a floating-point number
o Double monthlyPayment
```

Data types allow a computer to validate values inserted into each of the {{variable}} placeholders (e.g., `2.5` is a valid `{{rate}}` but `January` isn't). In other words, the Concerto data model allows a computer to make sense of the structure of (and data in) the clause. To learn more about data types see Concerto Modeling[27].

The clause data (the 'deal points') can then be captured as a machine-readable representation:

```
{
    "$class": "org.accordproject.interests.TemplateModel",
    "clauseId": "cec0a194-cd45-42f7-ab3e-7a673978602a",
    "loanAmount": 100000.0,
    "rate": 2.5,
    "loanDuration": 15
    "monthlyPayment": 667.0
}
```

The values entered into the template text are associated with the name of the variable e.g. `{{rate}}` = 2.5%. This provides the structure for understanding the clause and its contents.

Contract Assembly Logic

The clause below is a variant of the earlier fixed rate loan[32]. While it is consistent with the previous one, the `{{monthlyPayment}}` variable is replaced with a general purpose language expression `monthlyPaymentFormula(loanAmount,rate,loanDuration)` which calculates the monthly interest rate based upon the values of the other variables: `{{loanAmount}}`, `{{rate}}`, and `{{loanDuration}}`.

```
This is a *fixed interest* loan to the amount of
{{loanAmount}} at a yearly interest rate of {{rate}}% with a
loan term of {{loanDuration}},
and monthly payments of {{%
monthlyPaymentFormula(loanAmount,rate,loanDuration) %}}.
```

Contract Definition Logic

Contract definition logic for this template would calculate how much of the loan was outstanding, based on repayment events. Contract definition logic can be written in the user's language of choice. Accord Project currently supports converting Concerto models to many target languages, providing flexibility in language choice for Contract Logic.

Of course, many contracts have much more complex data relationships and calculations. Thankfully, the design of Accord Project Templates is extensible to more advanced scenarios too.

Progressive Adoption of Smart Legal Contracts

The combination of machine-readable text, data and machine-executable template and contract logic is collectively referred to as an *Accord Project Template* (Figure 3). The template artefact packages together the component parts in a standardized way.

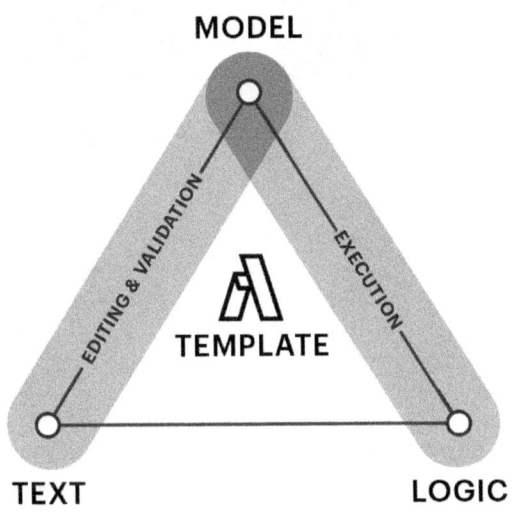

Figure 3: The Accord Project Template "triangle"

Although the template contains three core components (Text, Model & Logic), not all are necessary to demonstrate value. Often adoption occurs in an incremental way as organisation maturity and confidence increase (Figure 4).

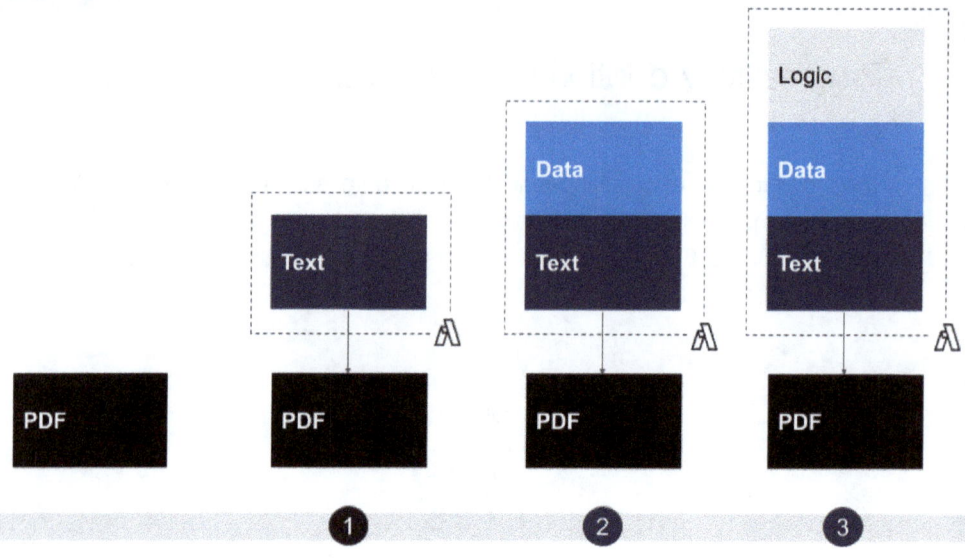

Figure 4: Progressive adoption of Accord Project Templates

Step 1 - Text Only

The first step of adoption often begins with Contract Text only. For example, online contract template services provide standard document text, or clauses that can be directly converted to Accord Project templates.

Accord Project templates can be used for this use-case by omitting the data and logic component entirely. The text of the template is completely static; there are no calculations, no dynamic rendering, and no placeholders for variables. Converting existing Clause libraries to Accord Project templates allows parity with existing contract authoring, negotiation, execution, and dispute resolution systems, that are extensible to more advanced stages as the organisation and use cases demand.

Furthermore, having a basis in a neutral rich-text format gives independence from specific document formats (such as Microsoft Word, Adobe PDF, RTF, HTML) but retains the option of rendering for a particular channel or file-type later on.

Finally, Accord Project templates can be cryptographically signed by their authors to demonstrate the provenance of their content.

Step 2 - Text + Data

In the next phase of maturity, we closely mirror the capabilities of document assembly solutions. The contract text can contain placeholders for values and authors can use those values to build templates that are dynamic. Sections of templates can be conditionally hidden, for example depending on the contract value, or jurisdiction. Also, sections become more reusable because they can be customized to individual circumstances without resorting to changing the approved text.

However, unlike traditional templating or document assembly systems, Accord Project templates use structured data modelling to give meaning to deal terms, reference data and parameters. For example, a system can understand whether a field called "state" refers to the residence of a party, the location of a property in a lease agreement, or the jurisdiction of a regulator.

Step 3 - Text + Data + Logic

In the third phase, we begin to realize the value of true computable smart legal contracts. As contracts become smarter, we can use more advanced logic to build more complex templates. Accord Project templates employ type-safe principles for template logic to help catch errors early and avoid embarrassing issues at signature.

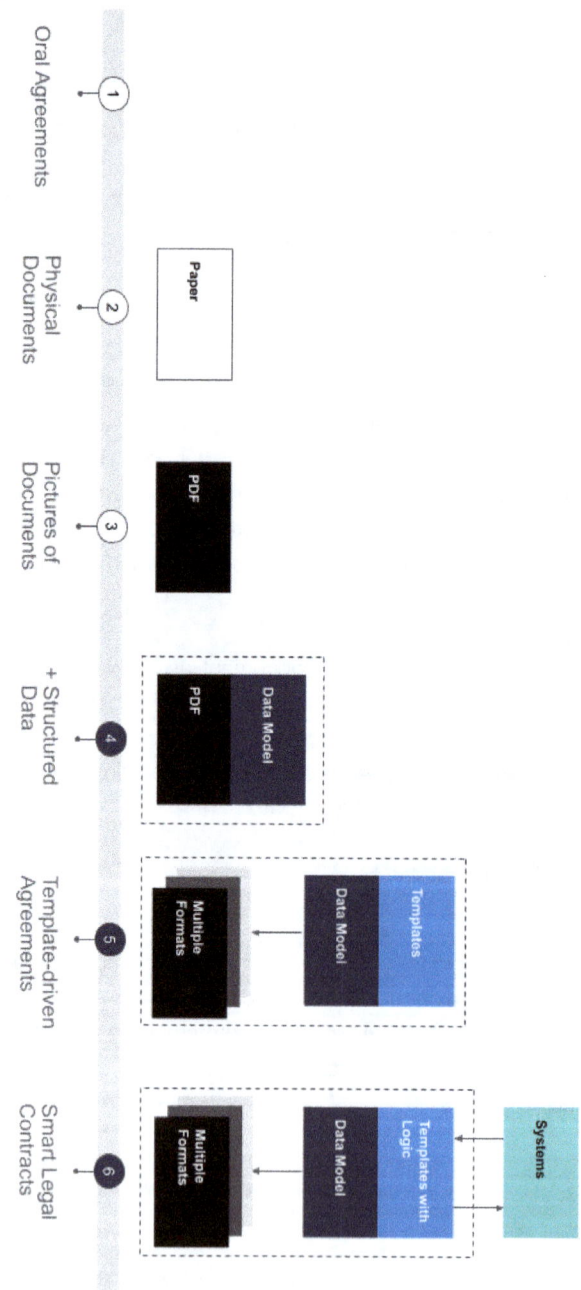

Figure 5: Smart Legal Contract maturity model

Evolution of Digital Agreements

The adoption of smart-legal contracts is a logical progression of contract maturity. Each phase is an opportunity to codify contract text, data, and logic across parties in an open, transparent, and accessible manner.

The contract maturity model (Figure 5) illustrates how contracts move from informal verbal agreements, to physical documents, to machine-readable documents, to active participants in business processes and systems.

Stage 4, 5 & 6 are phases of progressive adoption of Smart Legal Contracts. Each phase is described in more detail in the section, Progressive Adoption of Smart Legal Contracts.

System integration is relevant in multiple stages of adoption (for example in document assembly, supporting negotiation, or document storage). In Stage 6, the Smart Legal Contracts can also enable active integration post-signature. The conceptual boundary for the contract is illustrated by the dashed box.

Design Decisions

This section summarizes the motivations for the high-level design decisions in the technical implementation of Accord Project templates.

Describing Natural Language Templates

The natural language text for Accord Project templates is written in *TemplateMark*, an extension of Markdown. Markdown was chosen as the format for the natural language of a contract because it is a lightweight, textual format, focused on semantics rather than layout or styling, with broad industry cross-platform adoption and an open specification[33].

TemplateMark is itself defined using a Concerto data model[34] and can be represented as both Markdown text, and as a JSON object, with libraries that can convert from one format to another.

TemplateMark JSON is a well-defined file format, meaning that powerful template editors can be created to define it: including widgets and user experiences for defining conditional sections and formulae, and offering template preview and integrated testing. Template editing is closer to programming in our opinion than word processing and benefits from tools that go far beyond those offered by typical word processors. This flexibility allows a markdown template to be created that is used to create HTML, PDF or DOCX. One can even imagine using DOCX templates to create HTML or PDF files, or other scenarios.

Achieving Template Safety

Accord Project's template engine breaks the coupling between the template input format and the engine output format, and moves data format conversion outside of the core template engine.

Templates at the engine level are TemplateMark JSON documents and the output from the template engine is an *AgreementMark* JSON document. Separate libraries are used to convert source templates into TemplateMark JSON, or to render AgreementMark JSON to an output format.

Given the ability for templates to contain assembly logic there is an imperative to ensure that the templates are safe - i.e. when a template is merged with well-structured data it is guaranteed to produce a well-structured output. Too many templating engines fail in unpredictable ways at runtime, or silently generate invalid outputs when presented with data — unacceptable for enterprise usage.

Accord Project templates are therefore strongly-typed. The logic in templates is expressed in TypeScript. TypeScript is a strongly-typed, general purpose programming language, supported by a vibrant Open Source and enterprise community. TypeScript compiles to JavaScript for easy execution on most platforms.

The rich-text with variables of a template is associated with a Concerto data model. The Concerto data model defines the structure of the data required for the template, and is used to statically compile the template and verify type-safety. It is also used at runtime to ensure that incoming data is well structured.

Templates may be statically compiled to TypeScript programs, enforcing type-safety, ensuring that no unsafe code evaluation ("eval") is required at runtime, and easing integration into applications.

👁 Read more about the template compiler[35].

Describing Contract Data

Contracts include data points: the names of parties, addresses, details of purchased products, insurance provisions, warranties, expiration dates etc. To make contract data points machine-readable a data model representation is required. Given Accord Project's platform neutral goals, this data model must be usable across platforms. In addition, to allow computation over the data points in a contract the data modelling language must be usable from a variety of runtime execution environments and programming languages.

The Concerto data modelling language is used to describe the structure of data in a contract. Concerto models can be converted to a wide variety of platform-specific data models, such as JSON Schema, TypeScript, C#, Java, Go etc.

> 👁 Read more about the features, goals and motivations for Concerto[28].

Describing Contract Definition Logic

Previously, Accord Project experimented with creating a domain specific language (DSL) for contract definition logic (called Ergo[36]). Instead, we now recommend the use of General Purpose Programming languages. This decision is multifaceted:

- The high costs of building and maintaining a DSL
- DSLs can present a barrier to entry to both legal professionals and engineers.
- Loss of access to existing technical skills, communities & resources, such as utility libraries.

We still believe that domain-specific languages have their place, however, the domain should dictate the language.

Community & Adoption

This section highlights recent published work by members of the Accord Project community.

Governance and Legal

In November 2021, the Law Commission concluded that the current legal framework in England and Wales is sufficiently robust and adaptable to be able to facilitate and support the use of smart legal contracts. This makes it clear that smart contracts are legally binding and enforceable agreements, and also sets out the rules for creating, executing, and interpreting smart contracts. In the Law Commission's report[13], an example Accord Project template is used as an illustrative example of a Smart Legal Contract.

Members of Accord Project contributed to the Smarter Contracts[37] project from LawTech UK that explored potential benefits of areas such as smart legal contracts. LawTech UK's report on Smarter Contracts showcased an example of transfer of ownership of electronic trade documents using an NFT based on Accord Project technology.

Accord Project contributed to the International Organization for Standardization ISO/TR 23455:2019(en)[38] publication "overview of and interactions between smart contracts in blockchain and distributed ledger technology systems". Accord Project is highlighted as the first example of the role of domain specific languages and methods.

Niall Roche and Alastair Moore are also contributing to a working group at International Organization for Standardization ISO/IEC JTC 1/SC 29/WG 1[51] outlining the use of smart legal contracts as part of Media Asset Tokenization.

Commercial

Clause Inc. pioneered commercial implementations of the Accord Project stack through their cloud platform for smart agreements. Clause Inc was acquired by DocuSign[39] in May 2021. DocuSign continues to integrate Accord Project components into its Intelligent Agreement Management offerings, with a particular focus on structured and connected data in agreements, and ongoing sponsorship of Accord Project.

Open Terms Archive[40] uses the Accord Project data transformation stack to convert PDF documents to markdown format for indexing and search.

beNEXT's[41] smartLegal platform is a mobile-friendly, web-based platform to host Accord Project compatible smart legal contracts with an initial focus on the Property industry in the state of Victoria, Australia. beNEXT adopts Accord Project templates for contract assembly.

Nikolay Vlasov from AWS demonstrated deployment of Accord Project templates on AWS using AWS Lambda and Amazon QLDB in a series of blog posts[42] and code samples.

Decombine's[43] platform provides services to its members to build open source Smart Legal Agreements. Decombine has an initial focus on public sector procurement contracts in Europe.

The Building Blocks[46] are actively developing implementations of Smart Legal Contracts utilising the Accord Project framework in their venture builder portfolio.

Research

A selection of academic & commercial research.

A joint team from National Taiwan Normal University, University College of London, & HSBC Business School, Peking University proposed a pipeline in their 2022 paper[21] to use several NLP models to automate the creation of Accord Project templates from source contracts.

Northwestern University & Adobe Research published a research paper[24] introducing an AI-extracted graph representation of contracts called the Obligation Logic Graph (OLG) at the ACM ICAIL'23 conference. The OLG is mapped to a computable representation using Accord Project templates.

Jason Allen and Peter Hunn released the book Smart Legal Contracts, Computable Law in Theory and Practice[10] in July 2022.
This academic text is the first interdisciplinary account of smart contracts from a leading group of judges, practitioners, computer scientists, and legal scholars and was published by Oxford University Press.

Niall Roche and Alastair Moore wrote two chapters referencing the use of smart legal contracts in the book Enabling the Internet of Value: How Blockchain Connects Global Businesses Future of Business and Finance[46] and have authored papers on the use of smart legal contracts in the area of real estate and construction[47][49][50]. They have contributed a section on smart legal contracts and Accord project to the UK Law Society report on Blockchain Legal-Regulatory Guidance.[48]

In 2024, Purva Gupta & Kumar Neeraj Jha from the Indian Institute of Technology Delhi explored a novel approach to the automation of delay accountability, compensation, and pricing[52] in the construction domain using Accord Project templates. This builds upon their 2023 paper where they demonstrate a decentralised and automated contracting system[53] for large construction projects.

Blockchain and Distributed Ledger Technology

Accord Project has a long history of close collaboration with various Blockchain and DLT communities, including Hyperledger and Corda. Concerto was initially developed by IBM as part of the Open Source Hyperledger Composer project and compilation of Concerto to Java was supported by the Corda community. The Accord Project community has also developed libraries to facilitate on-chain execution of the definition logic of SLCs via a Hyperledger Fabric Smart Contract.

Internships

Accord Project participated in Google Summer of Code (GSoC) in 2020, 2021 & 2024, helping students become familiar with contributing to open source software. In 2022, Accord Project hosted its own Accord Project Summer of Code (APSoC) for the same purpose.

During GSoC 2020, Aman Sharma created a Microsoft Word Add-in to allow users to interact with AP templates directly in Microsoft Word. Patrik Keller worked on WebAssembly support for AP templates.

During GSoC 2021, Kushal Kumar added a transformer to the existing transformation library to convert CiceroMark into OOXML and vice-versa. Eason Chen worked on a project for automatic identification and classification of contract data types with natural language processing. Sanket Shevkar worked on allowing template authors to sign and verify a template.

APSoC 2022 saw Mehmet Tokgöz creating a Cicero Server REST API, Ayman Nawaz creating an extension for VSCode on the web, and Tanya Chhabra adding table support to the markdown transformation library.

Conclusion

Smart Legal Contracts represent a fusion of text, data, and logic, making contracts active participants in business processes and systems.

We've delineated a six stage maturity model, and a three stage adoption path for smart legal contracts, emphasizing their integration into systems for various functions like document assembly, negotiation, and storage.

We address the importance of making contract data machine-readable through a data model, using the Concerto data modelling language. Additionally, we introduce the concept of template safety, which ensures well-structured output from templates. Accord Project's TemplateMark technology is highlighted for its ability to maintain template consistency and safety.

For contract logic, we begin to build a taxonomy of contract logic, differentiating the logic needed for contract definition, automation, and assembly.

Finally, we also review Accord Project's contribution to smart legal contract governance and commercial implementations, and Accord Project's role in academic research and community contributions, such as the Google Summer of Code, underscoring its importance in the evolving landscape of computable contracts.

Further Information

How to Get Involved

Adopt Open Source Libraries and Components

Accord Project software libraries and components are capable of being embedded or deployed in a number of ways including:

- A standalone set of software libraries that can be embedded in other software languages such as .NET, Java, JavaScript or Rust.
- Within a web page via JavaScript and TypeScript libraries.
- Being invoked via a command line.
- Being invoked via implementations of the Accord Project API.
- Via AWS using Lambda functions for the operation of the contract clauses.
- Being integrated into distributed ledger solutions such as Hyperledger Fabric and Corda.

Contribute to the Codebase

If you find a bug, or have a need for a new feature, create an issue or open a pull request to our repositories on github.com/accordproject.

- Access an open ecosystem with leading industry stakeholders and participants.
- Learn the foundations of open source technologies and how to develop smart agreements.
- Provide input on the development of the technology stack components — language, models, templating, and other tools.

Join a Working Group

Accord Project hosts special interest groups in response to community demand.

The Accord Project Technology Working Group develops Open Source code libraries and specifications driven by requirements from Accord Project consumers. The goal is to be able to capture the domain-specific legal and transactional knowledge within the industry in a form that is amenable to automated computation and to bootstrap an ecosystem of companies and organisations that share legal and contract data using well-defined formats that are developed using open tools and libraries.

The Technology Working group is currently working on the following projects:
- Template Archive: a specification and set of libraries for parameterized natural language, data models, and computable logic. Accord Project templates can be used to create reusable clause templates, allowing legal clauses to interact with data from the outside world, and to perform automated computation.
- Concerto: a lightweight and web-friendly data model specification used to formally capture domain specific data models.
- Concerto Tools: a set of tools to convert Concerto models to and from other formats.

In addition, the Technology Working group develops and maintains the following resources:

- Project documentation.
- Template Playground: a web-based environment to view and edit Accord Project templates.
- Template Library: a web-hosted library of Apache-2 licensed Accord Project templates.
- Model Repository: a web-hosted library of Apache-2 licensed Concerto models.

The Technology Working group meets weekly (Wednesday at 8am EST) and discusses a wide range of implementation and design issues related to all of its active projects.

The NLP Working group meets monthly to discuss the application of NLP/AI technology to Smart Legal Agreements.

We encourage technologists and legal professionals with a technical background to get involved.

Make an Individual Donation

You can make a donation[44] of any amount through the Linux Foundation and show your support for the growth and evolution of smart legal contract technology.

Become a Corporate Sponsor

Influence the direction of Accord Project, by having your engineers solve the problems that matter to your organisation. Otherwise, we welcome corporate donations[44] through the Linux Foundation to cover administration and running costs.

- Connect with the global Accord Project Community.
- Support the development and implementation of Accord Project.
- Inspire legal technology growth and educational efforts worldwide.

Glossary

Accord Project. The Accord Project is an open ecosystem enabling anyone to build smart agreements and documents on a technology neutral platform.

AgreementMark. A Concerto data model for a rich-text document with embedded variable values.

blockchain. A blockchain is a distributed ledger with growing lists of records (blocks) that are securely linked together via cryptographic hashes.

computable contract. A computable contract is one that is specified in sufficient detail to provide unambiguous answers to questions about compliance of clearly specified circumstances with the terms and conditions of the contract. See also Smart Legal Contract.

Concerto. A data modelling language and associated tools, maintained by Accord Project.

contract. A contract is an agreement by parties creating mutual obligations that are enforceable by law.

contract assembly logic. Business logic that determines how a contract is created from a template, for a specific party and business transaction.

contract automation logic. Business logic and IT system configurations that are used by a party to a contract to fulfil their obligations under a contract.

contract definition logic. Semantics and logical rules that are specified by the text of a contract.

distributed ledger technology (DLT). Distributed ledger technology (DLT) is a digital system for recording the transaction of assets in which the transactions and their details are recorded in multiple places at the same time. Unlike traditional databases, distributed ledgers have no central data store or administration functionality.

document assembly. The process of creating a document for a specific business transaction. Typically this involves creating a document template and then merging the template with transaction data.

domain specific language (DSL). A domain-specific language (DSL) is a computer language specialized to a particular application domain. This is in contrast to a general-purpose language (GPL), which is broadly applicable across domains.

JavaScript (JS). A computer programming language used to make websites and applications dynamic and interactive. It's unique because it can run directly in your browser, not just on a server. JavaScript is one of the most commonly used programming languages of the internet.

JavaScript Object Notation (JSON). An open standard file format and data interchange format that uses human-readable text to store and transmit data objects. JSON is a language-independent data format.

knowledge graph. A knowledge graph, also known as a semantic network, represents a network of real-world entities—such as objects, events, situations or concepts—and illustrates the relationship between them.

large language model (LLM). A large language model (LLM) is a type of artificial intelligence (AI) program that can recognize and generate text, among other tasks. LLMs are trained on huge sets of data — hence the name "large." LLMs are built on machine learning: specifically, a type of neural network called a transformer model.

Linux Foundation. The Linux Foundation provides a neutral, trusted hub for developers and organisations to code, manage, and scale open technology projects and ecosystems.

machine-learning (ML). A branch of artificial intelligence (AI) and computer science that focuses on using data and algorithms to enable AI to imitate the way that humans learn, gradually improving its accuracy.

Markdown. Markdown is a lightweight markup language that you can use to add formatting elements to plaintext text documents. Created by John Gruber in 2004, Markdown is now one of the world's most popular markup languages.

natural language processing (NLP). Combines computational linguistics—rule-based modelling of human language—with statistical and machine-learning models to enable computers and digital devices to recognize, understand, and generate text and speech.

open source. Refers to something people can modify and share because its design is publicly accessible.

retrieval augmented generation (RAG). A technique for enhancing the accuracy and reliability of generative AI models with facts fetched from external sources.

smart legal contract. A human-readable and machine-readable contract that is digital, consisting of natural language and computable components. Also known as a Computable Contract.

smart contract. Self-executing program that automates the actions required in an agreement or contract. Once completed, the transactions are trackable and irreversible.

TemplateMark. A Concerto data model for a rich-text document template, with placeholders for variables, locale-specific formatting, conditional logic, and formulae.

TypeScript. A strongly typed programming language that builds on JavaScript.

WebAssembly (WASM). A binary instruction format for a stack-based virtual machine. WASM is designed as a portable compilation target for programming languages, enabling deployment on the web for client and server applications.

References

1. Davis, Jared Quincy. "The Shift from Models to Compound AI Systems." *Berkeley AI Research*, 18 February 2024, https://bair.berkeley.edu/blog/2024/02/18/compound-ai-systems/. Accessed 20 March 2024.
2. Trinh, Trieu, and Thang Luong. "AlphaGeometry: An Olympiad-level AI system for geometry." *Google DeepMind*, 17 January 2024, https://deepmind.google/discover/blog/alphageometry-an-olympiad-level-ai-system-for-geometry/. Accessed 20 March 2024.
3. *Accord Project*, https://accordproject.org. Accessed 20 March 2024.
4. *Linux Foundation - Decentralized innovation, built with trust*, https://www.linuxfoundation.org. Accessed 20 March 2024.
5. "Closing the Contract Gap in Sales Quoting." *DocuSign*, 2 December 2020, https://www.docusign.com/blog/closing-the-contract-gap-sales-quoting. Accessed 20 March 2024.
6. *Poor Contract Management Costs Companies 9% - Bottom Line*, 2012, https://www.worldcc.com/Resources/Content-Hub/details/Poor-Contract-Management-Costs-Companies-9-Bottom-Line. Accessed 20 March 2024.
7. *Recapturing Millions of Dollars by Leak-Proofing Your Contract Processes*, 8 May 2018, https://s3.eu-central-1.amazonaws.com/iaccmportal/resources/files/10151_iaccm-elevatewebinar-leak-proofingyourcontractprocesses-8may18.pdf. Accessed 20 March 2024.
8. McBride, Geraldine. "Global trade still depends on 4 billion paper documents daily. The U.K. is trying to change that." *Fortune*, 2 October 2023, https://fortune.com/2023/10/02/global-trade-4-billion-paper-documents-daily-uk-document-act-law-finance-geraldine-mcbride/. Accessed 20 March 2024.
9. *Legal Hackers* |, https://logalhackers.org/. Accessed 20 March 2024.

10. Allen, Jason, and Hunn, Peter, editors. *Smart Legal Contracts: Computable Law in Theory and Practice*. Oxford University Press, 2022. Accessed 20 March 2024.
11. Goodson, Nick, and Rongfei Lu. "CodeX - Programs and Centers - Stanford Law School." *Stanford Law School*, https://law.stanford.edu/codex-the-stanford-center-for-legal-informatics/. Accessed 20 March 2024.
12. "CodeX: Computable Contracts and Insurance · MIT Computational Law Report." *MIT Computational Law Report*, https://law.mit.edu/codex-computable-contracts-and-insurance. Accessed 20 March 2024.
13. "Smart contracts." *Law Commission*, https://lawcom.gov.uk/project/smart-contracts/. Accessed 20 March 2024.
14. "Smart Legal Contracts are recognised as being legally enforceable in England and Wales." *Accord Project*, 21 February 2023, https://accordproject.org/news/smart-legal-contracts-are-recognised-as-being-legally-enforceable-in-england-and-wales/. Accessed 20 March 2024.
15. Halford, Martin. "What are smart legal contracts?" *Accord Project*, 13 September 2021, https://accordproject.org/news/what-are-smart-legal-contracts/. Accessed 20 March 2024.
16. *OneNDA*, https://onenda.org. Accessed 20 March 2024.
17. *Common Paper: Build, negotiate, and sign contracts in minutes.*, https://commonpaper.com. Accessed 20 March 2024.
18. "Common Form · GitHub." *GitHub*, https://github.com/commonform. Accessed 20 March 2024.
19. *Standard Draft – Accelerating the process of reaching agreement*, https://www.standarddraft.com. Accessed 20 March 2024.
20. *Docassemble*, https://docassemble.org/. Accessed 20 March 2024.
21. Chen, Eason et al. *Conversion of Legal Agreements into Smart Legal Contracts using NLP*, 27 August 2022, https://arxiv.org/abs/2210.08954. Accessed 20 March 2024.
22. *Finchbot (Beta)*, https://finchbot.net/. Accessed 20 March 2024.

23. Selman, Dan. *Text Oriented Programming*, https://blog.selman.org/2023/08/07/text-oriented-programming/#more-2549. Accessed 20 March 2024.
24. Sergio, Servantez et al. *Computable Contracts by Extracting Obligation Logic Graphs*, 6 January 2023, https://dl.acm.org/doi/10.1145/3594536.3595162. Accessed 20 March 2024.
25. "The Use of Large Language Models in LegalTech." *Legaltech Hub*, 18 February 2023, https://www.legaltechnologyhub.com/contents/the-use-of-large-language-models-in-legaltech/. Accessed 20 March 2024.
26. "Frequently Asked Questions." *Accord Project*, https://accordproject.org/frequently-asked-questions/#smart-legal-contract. Accessed 20 March 2024.
27. *Concerto Documentation*, https://concerto.accordproject.org. Accessed 20 March 2024.
28. "Why Concerto? | Concerto." https://concerto.accordproject.org/docs/why-concerto. Accessed 20 March 2024.
29. *GitHub accordproject/template-engine*, https://github.com/accordproject/template-engine. Accessed 20 March 2024.
30. Selman, Dan. *ICAIL 2023: Workshop of Computable Contracts*, https://blog.selman.org/2023/06/20/icail-2023-computable-contracts-workshop/. Accessed 20 March 2024.
31. Selman, Dan. "Taxonomy of contract logic." *DocuSign*, 26 January 2024, https://www.docusign.com/blog/developers/taxonomy-contract-logic. Accessed 20 March 2024
32. *Accord Project Template Library - Fixed Rate Loan*, https://templates.accordproject.org/fixed-interests-static@0.2.0.html. Accessed 20 March 2024.
33. *CommonMark*, https://commonmark.org. Accessed 20 March 2024.

34. *Accord Project Model Repository - TemplateMark*, https://models.accordproject.org/markdown/templatemark@0.5.0.html. Accessed 20 March 2024.
35. *GitHub - accordproject/template-compiler*, https://github.com/accordproject/template-compiler. Accessed 20 March 2024.
36. Roche, Niall et al. *Ergo -- a programming language for Smart Legal Contracts*, 13 December 2021, https://arxiv.org/abs/2112.07064. Accessed 20 March 2024.
37. "Reports - LawtechUK." *LawtechUK*, https://lawtechuk.io/programmes/smarter-contracts. Accessed 20 March 2024.
38. "ISO/TR 23455:2019(en) Blockchain and distributed ledger technologies — Overview of and interactions between smart contracts in blockchain and distributed ledger technology systems." *ISO*, https://www.iso.org/obp/ui/#iso:std:iso:tr:23455:ed-1:v1:en. Accessed 20 March 2024.
39. "Taking the Next Step in Our Smart Agreement Journey." *DocuSign*, 28 May 2021, https://www.docusign.com/en-gb/blog/clause-docusign-smart-agreement-journey. Accessed 20 March 2024.
40. *Open Terms Archive*, https://opentermsarchive.org. Accessed 20 March 2024.
41. *beNEXT: Smart Legal Contracts*, https://www.benext.io/. Accessed 20 March 2024.
42. Vlasov, Nikolay *Verify delivery conditions with the Accord Project and Amazon Quantum Ledger Database – Part 1*, AWS, https://aws.amazon.com/blogs/database/verify-delivery-conditions-with-the-accord-project-and-amazon-quantum-ledger-database-part-1/. Accessed 20 March 2024.
43. *Combine DAO | Home*, https://combinedao.com. Accessed 20 March 2024.
44. LFX Crowdfunding, Accord Project, https://crowdfunding.lfx.linuxfoundation.org/projects/accordproject. Accessed 27 March 2024.
45. The Building Blocks https://www.thebuildingblocks.com Accessed 27 March 2024.
46. Vadgama, Nikhil, Xu Jiahua, Tasca Paolo, editors. *Enabling the Internet of Value How Blockchain Connects Global Businesses*. Chapter: *Real Estate and the Internet of*

Value (Alastair Moore, Niall Roche, Nikhil Vadgama) Pages 67-84. Chapter: *Oracles and Internet of Things in the Internet of Value* (Roche Niall, Moore Alastair) Pages 157-174. ISBN 10.1007/978-3-030-78184-2

47. Roche Niall, Moore Alastair, *Oraclised Data Schemas: Improving contractual certainty in uncertain times* https://www.academia.edu/93413773/Oraclised_Data_Schemas_Improving_contractual_Certainty_in_uncertain_Times?uc-sb-sw=5516813. Accessed 27 March 2024.

48. The Law Society, Blockchain Legal Regulatory Guidance (Second Edition) https://prdsitecore93.azureedge.net/-/media/files/topics/research/blockchain-legal-and-regulatory-guidance-second-edition-2022.pdf?rev=d15fe95a00ca4d179b7d6df97950fd5a&hash=14133E112A070BBEAE2A1D342B6DC61A. Accessed 27 March 2024.

49. Construction Blockchain Consortium CBC 2021/2022/2023 presentation by Alastair Moore and Niall Roche. https://doi.org/10.47330/CBC.2022.WQWU1576 https://www.constructionblockchain.org/proceedings-2021 Accessed 27 March 2024.

50. Towards a distributed ledger of residential title deeds in the UK, https://discovery.ucl.ac.uk/id/eprint/10160676/1/HMLR%20White%20Paper.pdf. Accessed 27 March 2024.

51. ISO/IEC JTC 1/SC 29, Coding of audio, picture, multimedia and hypermedia information, https://www.iso.org/committee/45316.html. 27 March 2024.

52. Purva Gupta & Kumar Neeraj Jha, *Determining Delay Accountability, Compensation, and Price Variation Using Computable Smart Contracts in Construction*, https://doi.org/10.1061/JMENEA.MEENG-58. Accessed 27 March 2024.

53. Purva Gupta & Kumar Neeraj Jha,. *A Decentralized and Automated Contracting System Using a Blockchain-Enabled Network of Stakeholders in Construction Megaproject*, https://doi.org/10.1061/JMENEA.MEENG-5366. Accessed 27 March 2024.

www.ingramcontent.com/pod-product-compliance
Lightning Source LLC
Chambersburg PA
CBHW051204170526
45158CB00005B/1819